Contents

Preface

What's spiritual warfare then? The things of this world around us are caused and affected by angels, demons, and God's people, as part of a cosmic fight. It's huge. It might sound... peculiar... but when we've accepted 'God' as one Spirit living in a realm beyond our sight, it follows that there may well be other spirits (small 's') to be aware of. So here is our battle plan: 1. Know your enemy. It's not as simple as "God vs. devil". "The accuser" = "Satan" in the original Hebrew isn't God's equal. God created everything, including Lucifer (the story goes that Lucifer was a good angel before he rebelled against God and became Satan), and God has ultimate power over everything. God allows Satan to exist and to act (Job 1:12), for reasons of love and freedom of choice that we can trust are best in the long run, but if Satan tried to take on God directly, there'd be no contest (check Revelation 12:7-9). So, his "indirect" attacks on God = attacks on His precious children. Yes, us. Satan's out to destroy the things, and the people, of God. But. Whilst it's true that this needs to be taken seriously (what needs to be taken seriously is our relationship to God) - HE IS STRONGER. What now? In war, clever lies are more valuable than face-to-face fights. Don't be surprised if the situation you're in seems like Satan's far more powerful. It's not true: powerful lies are his strategy. The oldest known Christian creed is "Jesus is Lord". In every place of fear or despair you find yourself in, speak that out to the darkness, over and over - it's more scared of that truth than you are of it.

Now, the enemy is identified. Now there's good news coming... 2. Know the battlefield. It's you. God loves you, and wants you to know it. Satan wants to separate you from Him. The battle is over you. Your actions (which Satan can use to claim you) are based in your words, your words in your thoughts. This is one reason why praising God is so powerful: you're focusing on Him in your mind, AND you're welcoming Him into your mind. That's an impenetrable cloud of beauty, that you were made for, and Satan can't get near.

3. Know your protection. The biggest and best protection you have is, simply, JESUS and HIS BLOOD. When you've said "yes" to Jesus, His blood set you free from any "they sinned and now I own them!" claim that Satan had on you. You're not in his power. You're not in his kingdom. You're in Christ, with all the freedom, the love, the peace of mind and the deepest joy that the "armour of God" is all about.

This isn't a blueprint for you to charge into Satan's kingdom, SAS style, and rescue hostages. Except... Remember how the battlefield is you? By getting your relationship with God sorted, choosing against sin, and by wanting to see other people come to know that Jesus is for them (Romans 8:31), you're storming the most important of strongholds.

What now? Ephesians 6:1-10 is a famous passage on the work that Jesus has done for you. We'd suggest you commit to pray to re-position yourself into that armour every day. Then take that freedom that Christ brings. As you read and study these 13 Lessons you shall become stronger and ground in Christ.

FIGHT THE <u>GOOD</u> FIGHT OF FAITH

KEY TEXT: HEBREW 11:1,6

THE FULL ARMOR

Therefore, put on the full armor of God, so that when the day of
Evil comes, you may be able to stand your ground. Ephesians 6:13

DEMONS are spiritual enemies and it is the responsibility of each Christian to deal with them directly in spiritual warfare. Demon spirits can invade and indwell human bodies. It is their objective to do so. By indwelling a person they obtain a greater advantage in controlling that person than when they are working from the outside. When demons indwell a person, that person is said to have evil spirits or to be possessed with demons. The word translated "possessed" by the KJV should be translated "demonized" or "have demons." Much misunderstanding has resulted from the used of the word "possessed." This word suggests TOTAL OWNERSHIP. **In this sense a Christian could never be "demon possessed".** He could not be OWNED by demons, because he or she is owned by Christ.

THE SHIELD OF FAITH

"In addition to all this take up the shield of faith, with which you can extinguish all the flaming arrows of the evil one." Ephesians 6: 16

While we have walked in IGNORANCE and DARKNESS the enemy has SUCCESSEFLLY made inroads into each of us. We must now learn how to GET him out and how to KEEP him out. His work must be resisted. When assaulted from without, we can bind our minds to the mind of Christ, take responsibility for our actions and walk according to the guidelines of scripture. Example: suppose you hear a thought whispered to your mind, "So-and-so thinks you are stupid." Demons talk to our minds like that. This is one of the ways they plant seeds of resentment and suspicion. You can soon learn to distinguish between what is of SELF, of GOD or of SATAN. If it is of SELF, a positive affirmation may solve the problem. If it is of God, pray for understanding and clarity. If it is of Satan, rebuke him. You might say: *"You are a liar, demon. I reject that thought about my friend. My mind is under the protection of the blood of Jesus. I bind you from my thoughts. I bind my mind to the mind of Christ and I loose my mind from any thoughts coming from you. I command you to leave me alone, in the name of Jesus."* THIS IS AN EXAMPLE OF RESISTING THE DEVIL.

THE SWORD OF THE SPIRIT

The sword of the Spirit, is a reminder that the battle is spiritual, and must be fought in
God's strength, depending on the word and on God through prayer.

Be honest with yourself. Ask God to help you see where and how demons may have invaded your life. This does not mean to mull over past sins and unpleasant things in the past. It is simply recognizing that demons have TAKEN ADVANTAGE of the SINS and *CIRCUMSTANCES* in life. In order for those intruders to be driven out they have to be recognized for who they are, AND THE DOORS CLOSED BEHIND THEM.

Begin to practice self-deliverance. Pick out areas in your life where you know demons are troubling you, and command them to come out in Jesus' name. Luke 10:17-19. When the demons see that you are absolutely renouncing them and are SPEAKING IN FAITH, they will respond. Do not let them go unchallenged another day. Claim your heritage as listed in Romans 14:17.

In many homes today, even though husband, wife and children may profess Christ, there is strife, division, confusion and chaos. It is time the devil took his share of the blame. And it is time families learn how to drive the devil out of their homes. The ideal starting point for victory is for each member of the family to commit himself anew to Jesus Christ. This should be followed by deliverance for each one. (In one church, the men led out in rededication and receiving deliverance). When the whole family is cooperating and considering one another, the devil is defeated in a hurry.

If you are the only one in your home willing to receive deliverance, you should still proceed. After receiving your deliverance you are then better able to enter into spiritual warfare against the demons that are controlling the lives of your family and friends. You are better able to intercede for their blindness to be removed. 2 Corinthians. 4:3,4.

WARFARE IS NOT PRAYER! **IT IS IN ADDITION TO PRAYER.** There is no point of petitioning God for something He has already given you. God has given us power and authority OVER THE DEVIL. We must not expect God to get the devil off our backs. He has already defeated Satan and given us the ability and responsibility to take care of ourselves. God has given us the WORD, ARMOUR, THE BLOOD and the name of JESUS We can either spend our time begging God for what is already ours, or we can start receiving what He has already given to us.

Sample prayer:

You demons that are troubling _____ we take authority over you in the mighty name of Jesus. You are seeking to destroy this home, but we will not permit you to do so. We are seated together with Christ in spiritual authority. We know our position and our rights. We bind you in Jesus' name. Take your hands off of _____ life. Release _____ will that he/she may be free to accept Christ as Savior and receive deliverance.

THE HELMET OF SALVATION

Take the helmet of Salvation and the sword of the Spirit, which is the word of God.
And pray in the Spirit on all occasions with all kinds of prayers and requests. With
This in mind, be alert and always keep on praying. Ephesians 6: 17,18

All spiritual battles do not end quickly and victoriously, but you will see enough victories to know that spiritual warfare makes an amazing difference. Sometimes all that is missing is spiritual warfare. Some battles will take longer than others. Spiritual warfare *DOES NOT CONTROL THE WILL OF THE PERSON.* It simply BINDS the power of demon forces, and releases the will to make decisions without demon interference. Demons *are* not cast out of the person, but their power is bound for a season. This type of warfare is in full accordance with spiritual principles set forth in Corinthians. 10:3 & Eph. 6:12. These passages teach that our warfare is against *spiritual* enemies and must be fought with *spiritual* weapons. It is useless and wrong to be drawn into flesh to flesh encounters.

It should be the aim of every home to maintain God's pattern of divine authority wives submitting to husbands, husbands loving their wives as Christ loved the church, and children obeying their parents in the Lord. This will reduce the devil's opportunities to a minimum in any home.

"Healing and Holiness"

Key text: Luke 4:18,19 and Eph 4:24

There is a strong need among our membership and friends, for healing and holiness, only God can do this great work in our lives. Let's take a closer look.

Sin is more than the wrong things we do. It is the motivations and forces that push us to do wrong. Sin is what we know is wrong and what pushes or pulls us into evil, even though we are unconscious of the source. Sin is also progressive. We do not wake up one day and decide to commit adultery. We stew in pain and frustration and misery for a while, and try various ways to find satisfaction and relief. If we do not discover a new source of strength, power and commitment, we fall further along the pathway of sin. So, sin is not only what we do but it can also be the lack of what we need that places us in a position of starvation.

Sin can be termed **accumulated FRUSTRATION that we try to resolve in ways that are contrary to the will of God.** If we only see sin as the VISIABLE actions and not the INVISABLE motivations and driving forces, we will be quick to discipline those who have fallen into sin without addressing the root causes. PLEASE KEEP IN MIND, THERE ARE NO EXCUSES FOR SIN. SIN IS WRONG AND SIN IS SIN WHETHER YOU ARE FRUSTRATED OR NOT. However, if all we do is concentrate on the commands not to sin, and overlook the ROOT causes for our sins, we will stop sinning one way (when that sin becomes public or unpleasant to us) and start sinning another way (just to relieve the pressure). We will have worked on the SYMPTOM of the problem and not the SOURCE of the problem.

Confession of sin is necessary, not to convince God to forgive us, but rather to alert our minds and hearts to our desperate need for God. God floods our hearts with the truth that He is the ONLY one who can heal our past. He is the ONLY one who can heal us in a way that we will stop repeating the same mistakes and hurting ourselves, and others. When you come to the understanding that God loves you and wants to free you from your mess, you can then BECOME WHOLE and HEALTHY.   Health and Wholeness are definitions of holiness.

Holiness is not just about avoiding what is EVIL and OLD but it is also about what is GOOD and NEW. We are SEPERATED FROM evil but are SET APART for that which is good. (Surely goodness and mercy SHALL FOLLOW ME).   If holiness was strictly separation from Evil we would already be in Heaven. That is not what God wants right now, for some reason God wants us here.

God wants us to live holy in this present world. He left us here to become a Holy nation. He has a mission to accomplish. The holiness cannot be accomplished on our own merit. The bible clearly states, "We are, SINFUL, CARNAL AND SOLD UNTO SIN." Paul is right, "God who works within us both to will, and to do of His good pleasure." Phil 2:13

If God does not provide inner healing for the INVISIBLE wounds, the people who desire to live in holiness will come under bondage to old things. If inner healing is not available to those who are seeking to consecrate their lives to the Lord, they will never fully develop their ministries and gifts. Their unhealed wounds from the past will reach into the present and hold them back.

For example, a pastor may be completely consecrated to the Lord, working and straining to win people to Christ. God moves and many people join the church. Then the unhealed wounds in the life of that pastor will begin to manifest themselves through hard attitudes toward those people. And one day, the people may leave. The pastor becomes discouraged, which causes the level of his consecration to diminish. The evangelist who never felt valued nor received *recognition* from his parents during these formative years may become raised up and anointed by God with a powerful ministry with signs and wonders. One day he finds that the flow seems to be blocked. He doesn't realize that lately he has been trying to heal his NEED FOR APPROVAL through his work. He makes himself the center of attention instead of giving glory to God.

Our final example is of a Prayer Warrior dedicated to spiritual warfare may suddenly have to abandon the battle because the devil penetrated her rearguard, and destroyed her marriage - all because there were UNRESOLVED issues in her own emotions. She refused to see what was happening, and never dealt with those invisible wounds

In order for conversion to happen and its marvelous effects remain, HEALING IS NECESSARY. Healing is the Lord plugging up and repairing the holes in your soul before filling you with His spirit. This is to be our DAILY experience. 1 Corinthians. 1:2. As we continue TO GROW in our commitment to the Lord, we will receive understanding of hidden levels of NEW THINGS in our lives that need to be healed. The Lord heals some situations instantly. Like the woman with the issue of blood, just one touch, and she was healed. Luke8: 46-48. The woman at the well, the Lord healed her instantly of her psychological problems. John 4.

Others need a PROCESS of ministry and healing that is more involved. If we have been healed in ONE AREA of our life and not in others, those other areas will become sources of FRUSTRATION and SIN and stumbling blocks to holiness.

We come to God in order to be born again. But after we become children of God we often start planning how to TRY HARD ENOUGH TO NOT SIN without God's help. Many good believers say, "I don't need inner healing and deliverance because I already received everything from God in my CONVERSION. I am a new creature, old things have passed away." The only problem is THEIR LIVES DON'T RESEMBLE THAT OF JESUS IN ATTITUDE AND ACTION. 2 Corinthians. 5:17 is really saying that the old things are passing away and all things are being made new. This is a process; it is an attitude change. The Holy Spirit shows us that we need to be MORE LIKE Christ in thought, relationships, actions and motivations. He also reveals that there are some things from our past that still plagues and color our present. We need to be healed and delivered from those things.

One of the problems we face in the church is the struggle to be pure without the healing of our wounds. The bible says that we are covered with WOUNDS and bruises and PURTREFYING SORES. To demand holiness without healing of the wounds is to invite more guilt and frustration. Mark 1:21-35. The demonized man had been lead to church to divert the attention of the people away from Christ. But Christ, casting out the demons, brought back all the attention to him. Based upon this passage, the casting out of devils was a daily occurrence for Jesus, both in and out of the synagogue.

The SECRET cause of the affliction was in his life. He had been FASCINATED by some pleasure of sin. He became perverted along the way, and eventually was under another's control. He became helpless, and Satan tried to make him believe that he was hopeless. You are not hopeless. Jesus is here to help you and heal you. He died for the right and privilege of blessing you. As you experience an encounter with the healing power of the Lord, the basic needs or wants of your personality will be resolved. Remember only God can deal with your INVISIBLE wounds.

PRAYER IS AN ACT OF WAR

PART ONE

KEY TEXT: EPHESIANS 6:13-18

Our world is built around the concept of TERRITORIES. When God created Adam and Eve, He gave them a specific TERRITORIAL assignment. God called them to a specific task. Genesis 12:1-5 we read of the specific assignment that God gave to Abram. When God called the children of Israel to go in and possess the Promise Land, each tribe was given specific TERRITORIES to take dominion over.

Acts 1: 8. Notice the precise TERRITORIAL assignments. One area was to be secure before branching off into other areas. Home is our Jerusalem. Home is where our work begins. Home is where the most vicious fights will take place over spiritual TERRITORY. Matthew. 13:53-58.

God wants us to learn how to submit to leadership, to put our flesh under control, to be a servant and to mind the business of our specific TERRITORIES. The best place for that to begin and occur is in Jerusalem. Jerusalem is where God works on the kinks in our armor. Jerusalem is where they remember all our mistakes and slips as we grow in the Lord. Jerusalem is our first and foremost fiery furnace. The sooner in, the sooner out. Some of us spend vast amounts of time in the furnace because we refuse to learn our Jerusalem lessons.

Just as there are spiritual TERRITORIAL assignments, there are also spiritual SEASONS of ministry. Each season of ministry has a TRANSITION period. It is during these TRANSITION times that the enemy is most active. When you sense that a change is coming or is needed that is the time when you are most vulnerable to accepting a counterfeit. Usually right before God brings His best, the enemy offers us something good. Satan will try to get you to move TOO SOON or NOT AT ALL. Remember the story of Abraham and Isaac. God first said sacrifice Isaac. Then God said sacrifice the ram. What would have happened if Abraham had not understood the change of assignment?

We have to learn how to pray the prayer of AGREEMENT. The prayer of AGREEMENT is like the coordination of a symphony. When a symphony plays many instruments perform but they all play the same song. If you are in AGREEMENT you might pray a prayer like **"Father I agree with what my friend has asked You for this day. I thank you that Your Word declares 'that if two of you agree on earth concerning anything that they ask, it will be done for them by My Father in heaven.' Now, Father, according to your Word, I thank You for answered prayer. Your Word says that 'faith is the substance of things hoped for, the evidence of things not seen.' So I am praying with faith asking You to do these things now. In the name of Jesus, Amen."**

Sometimes in prayer we must break a Yoke. YOKES are spiritual oppressions and HEAVY LOADS that Satan puts on people in order to hold them in bondage. A simple prayer concerning breaking yokes is: **"In the name of Jesus, I thank You Father, that every yoke the enemy has put on (name) is being broken. Satan will no longer cause (him or her) to participate in sin. Lord I thank You that the blindness is falling off his/her eyes concerning this sin right now and that the glorious light and truth of Your Word is being revealed to (name).**

TEARING DOWN STRONGHOLDS. Strongholds are FORTIFIED PLACES that Satan builds to exalt himself against the knowledge and plans of God. 2 Corinthians. 10:3-5; Revelation 2:13. There are TERRITORIAL, IDEOLOGICAL and PERSONAL strongholds. Personal strongholds include your personal life, personal sins, your thoughts, feelings, attitudes and behavior patterns. A stronghold is a mindset, IMPREGNATED with hopelessness that causes the believer to accept as unchangeable, something that he/she knows is contrary to the will of God

SUPPLICATION and TRAVAIL. The word SUPLICATION means, *"to beg."* Acts 1:14. SUPPLICATON can be likened to a woman who is ready to have her baby at any moment. There is NO HOLDING back the birth. TRAVAIL is what happens when we begin to EXPERIENCE the pangs of childbirth. Gal. 4:19. There are counterfeits and false travails. Here are a few points to help you recognize the work of the Holy Spirit:

   a. Travail is given by God and is not something we can make happen. It is not something we should personally work up. There are those who try to make themselves travail, but God's moving on us is not something that can be turned off and on like a water faucet.
   b. Travail sometimes comes as a result of praying in an area that others have prayed about before you. God then chooses you to be one of the last prayers before the matter is accomplished. You are the one who gives birth to the answer.
   c. Many times travail can be so strong that it seems to overwhelm the intercessor. Those around need to intercede for the one in travail if this happens in a group situation. Travail is like giving birth and in a way we are acting as midwives when we assist those in travail. ONE WORD OF CAUTION. The Holy Spirit will rule over our emotions in a time of travail. We must be sure that we don't let our emotions run wild. We need to walk in the fruit of self-control

PRAYER IS AN ACT OF WAR

PART TWO

The LANGUAGE of Intercession

What do we mean when we speak of **SPIRITUAL WARFARE, STRONGHOLDS, BINDING THE EMEMY** and **PRAYING THE PRAYER OF AGREEMENT?** Many prayer groups lack real authority because they do not have proper teaching on the biblical meaning and application of the words they use in prayer. When prayer becomes empty talk, misunderstanding, misinterpretation and confusion are the results. 1 Corinthians. 1:10.

Matt. 18:18,19. & Amos 3:7. There are times when God will lead His children to pray for His will to be done in a particular situation. The word **agreement** in the Greek means "to be harmonious or symphonize." When a symphony plays, many instruments perform, each adding its own quality to the blend heard by the composer. In the same way God uses many types of prayers and people praying to orchestrate His divine melody of prayer. God does not place the responsibility or authority for His will to be done on earth on only one believer. This also shows how important it is to take OUR PLACE in prayer. We can help shoulder a burden that may be too much for someone else to bear alone. Little prayers help make up for what is lacking.

How many people does it take to pray until a certain need is met? The stronger the resistance or higher the territorial power, (Eph. 6:11,12) the more people may be required to break the stronghold. The answer also depends on the level of authority that the person praying has in the Spirit. This is not to say that every prayer counts or does not count, or that one is more important than the other. Veteran prayer warriors, those who have experienced God's moving many times in answer to prayer, sometimes will have a quick breakthrough when they stand in the gap for certain situations. This is because they believe wholeheartedly that God will move as they pray according to His will. There is an authority that comes with such prayers of faith, and the enemies of God know that they are in trouble when this authority rings out in a prayer meeting. In addition, Fasting multiplies the effect of prayer. Fasting will touch things that prayer alone will not affect.

How do I know when I have prayed enough? When you are no longer reminded repeatedly by the Holy Spirit to pray about a particular concern. If more prayer is needed God will prompt you to pray until His will has been accomplished. Sometimes the unction to pray for that particular situation is no longer felt. You may or may not see the answer in the natural but as far as God is concerned, He has what He desired to provide the answer in the spiritual realm. Remember we walk by faith and not by sight.

What does it mean to Break a Yoke? Genesis. 27:40 & Isaiah. 10:27. Yokes are spiritual oppressions and heavy loads that Satan put on people in order to hold them in bondage. In biblical times, **yokes** were made for a team of two oxen. A strong or lead ox would take the larger side and the younger, weaker ox the opposite side. The weaker ox **HAD TO PLOW** with the stronger ox. When we are in yoke with Christ, the burden is light because He is pulling the weight and making the way as the stronger one. **Satan** has **counterfeited this principle in** *order to put heavy yokes on people* to oppress them and bring them into bondage to sin, occult activities and wrong relationships. Samson had the yoke of Satan upon his neck. His flesh became the tool Satan used to bind, oppress, and depress. 2 Corinthians. 6:14.

How should we pray for those who are enslaved in a yoke?
a. Fast. Isaiah 58:6.
b. Pray a binding prayer against the power of sin, legalism, and occult practices. Forbid Satan from holding him or her in his grasp.
c. Command Satan to stop blinding his or her eyes to the glorious light of the Gospel. 2 Corinthians. 4:4
d. If a relationship with fornication or adultery exists, pray that the tie be broken. Pray a losing prayer wherein you command the people involved to be loosed from the wrong relationship. Fasting and prayer will be needed to break this yoke.
e. Praise God for the deliverance to come. Praise releases captives from their captivity. Psalm 149. Praise binds the king with chains.

Be sensitive to your seasons of ministry. God does not always call you to make a change because you have been wounded. You must always seek to find the motive behind your feelings about a certain situation. Many people make mistakes during transition periods of ministry and growth. Usually right before God brings His best, the enemy offers something that looks incredibly good. There are times to leave and times to come.

When we wait for God's time and leave or arrive in the right spirit we add to the unity of the family. You may feel that God has called you to assist another ministry, but have not been spiritually released to leave because your heart is not right or there is still some work for you to do or lessons to learn before you leave.

Consider the story of Abraham and Isaac. God asked Abraham to sacrifice his son. Then God said to spare Isaac and sacrifice instead, the ram in the thicket. Because of our urgent nature we would have probably killed Isaac and walked away from the ram never taking the time to hear from God or seek for His will. Be sure that you hear the voice of God and not the voice of another person. People who tell you to go here or go there may be anointed, but they may not know their own hearts. In making decisions it is important not to let human emotions get involved with the decision-making process. Obey God and not man.

RESTORATION TAKES TIME

PART ONE

KEY TEXT: EPH 4:24, 25

We come to God with POLUTTED minds and hearts. We are not who we appear to be. Sometimes we are not who we THINK we are. We are complex of feeling, memories, and behavior patterns influenced by conscious, sub-conscious and spiritual and biological forces. Therefore, our new position in Christ requires a thorough cleaning. This cleansing takes place through the washing of the word, worship, prayer and other spiritual *disciplines*. Eph. 4:22-32; *5:26;* Rom. 12:2;Titus 3:5.

When we FINALLY surrender to the Holy Spirit and turn our lives over to God, we usually are still filled with old attitudes, wrong patterns of thinking and strange Non-Biblical ideas. We often try to make God fit into our concept of religion. We MIX Bible truth with the errors of our personality. We create another tree of knowledge of good and evil. We hide from God and others while pretending to be real. Usually, we are only as real as we have surrendered. Those parts of us that are not yet under the full control of Christ remain under the cover of pretense. Our pretense eventually fails and we hang our heads in despair. We say, "God failed," when in reality, we failed to allow God to work through us and in us.

One popular false belief and concept about God is that "God will not love me if I fail." This wrong concept says that God leaves me every time I fail. Then I begin to punish myself for my failures by wallowing in guilt and shame as barriers to falling again. I do not accept God as a loving nurturing Father who is always ready to encourage my growth. Of course guilt and shame do not make one righteous. I fail again. The cycle repeats itself.

We struggle to know God better because after we have received FORGIVENESS and ETERNAL LIFE we still must live each day of our lives on this earth. What we see, hear, taste and feel all remind us of things we experience or have experienced in this life, both good and bad. We struggle with physical and spiritual hungers, emotional sorrows, loss, rejection ,rudeness, fear and other powerful feelings. The key to winning over these struggles lies in the understanding of JUSTIFICATION and SANCTIFICATION. JUSTIFICATION is GIVEN FOR YOU, and done FOR YOU, free of charge. Rom. 5. SANCTIFICATION is done IN YOU, You are COVERED BOTH WAYS. Heb. 10: 10-16; Phil.2:13.

Wrong choices may slow down your progress, but if you repent and allow the Holy Spirit to teach you, you will be placed back on track and start moving forward again. God can restart you with an unblemished, untarnished, 100 percent, still intact relationship. The forgiveness, grace and mercy of God will place your past under the blood. You are then free to let go of your past and leave it there. Regardless of what anyone tell you, God's plan and purposes for you are not limited or diminished because you messed up in the past. You are the only one who can limit your ability to receive God's grace, and YOU WILL ONLY CHOOSE TO LIMIT THE GRACE OF GOD IN YOUR LIFE IF YOU ARE HOLIDNG ON TO MENTAL, EMOTIONAL OR SPIRITUAL POLLUTION, because of some false concept of God or righteousness.

Rom. 10:4-13. This NEW BIRTH is a PROCESS. Satan also knows about the process, therefore he will attempt to get you to stop the process. When you surrender to Jesus you receive a new identity. You are FORGIVEN, SAVED, and walking with God. Satan moves quickly and often quietly to CHIP AWAY at your new identity. He attacks through the pulls of our flesh, feelings and focus of life.

As new believers, we are still in the flesh with "technical" new natures that are still being WORKED OUT and WORKED INTO our minds. The real trouble begins as we begin to grow spiritually. We have COVENANT RIGHTS. Part of the process is becoming LOOSED from Satan, his bondage and our personal hurts, pains and areas of non-forgiveness, which have now become new STRONGHOLDS.

In order to respond properly to your circumstances, your mind, will and emotions must be BOUND to the will of God and LOOSED FROM your wrong senses and emotions. With the RIGHT KEY you can LOCK yourself to Christ and UNLOCK yourself from your past. This will allow you to SUBMIT to His will and make the right choices.

Satan USES our wrong senses, emotions and ideas against us. We hide behind our personally acceptable errors, and they become STRONGHOLDS in our lives. We become BOUND to them. Our fears and past pains become doorways that Satan uses to attack and discourage us. We have held on to many positions and ideas from the past in our feeble effort to protect ourselves. We have believed and bought into the lie that we are UNLOVED, UNWANTED, UNCECESSARY, UNSUCCESSFUL, UNWORHTY, and SPIRITUALLY AND EMOTIONALLY UGLY. If in our hearts we believe these lies to be true, we will build a STRONGHOLD around them to protect them. We will become SUSPICIOUS of anyone trying to convince us that we have believed a lie. We even become suspicious of God and the truths of the Bible.

If you have built STRONGHOLDS around the painful issues of your life, Satan will use them to keep you away from continuing your PROCESS of Spiritual Growth. Satan knows about your unmet needs, unresolved memories, pain, anger, bitterness, unforgiveness and hidden sin. He will use these burdens to attack you.

The ROOT PROBLEMS is your DAMAGED HEART and the STRONGHOLDS you have built to protect it. Your barriers sometimes keep the pain out, but mostly they KEEP THE PAIN IN. THE QUESTION IS not do you have problems, but what are you going to do about them? God is not your problem. Your OLD NATURE is your problem. BINDING and LOOSING makes it possible to CRUCIFY that old nature and receive God's full healing and restoration. Matt. 16:1918:18.

RESTORATION TAKES TIME

PART TWO

Key text: EPH 4:24, 25

Restoration TAKES TIME. One popular false belief and concept about God is that "God will not love me if I fail." This wrong concept says that God leaves me every time I fail. Then I begin to punish myself for my failures by wallowing in guilt and shame as barriers to falling again. I do not accept God as a loving, nurturing Father who is always ready to encourage my growth. Of course guilt and shame do not make one righteous. I fail again. Then the cycle repeats itself.

We struggle to know God better because after we have received FORGIVENESS and ETERNAL LIFE, we still must live each day of our lives on this earth. What we see, hear, taste and feel, all remind us of things we experience or have experienced in this life, both good and bad. We struggle with physical and spiritual hungers, emotional sorrows, loss, rejection, rudeness, fear and other powerful feelings. The key to winning over these struggles, lies in the understanding of JUSTIFICATION and SANCTIFICATION. JUSTIHCATION is GIVEN FOR YOU, and done FOR YOU, free of charge. Rom. 5. SANCTIFICATION is done IN YOU, you are COVERED BOTH WAYS. Heb. 10:10-16; Phil. 2:13.

Too many people in the church see themselves in terms of their past. (Your past is only a record of your limitations WHILE BOUND, and not the SUCCESSES you will have in your FUTURE with Christ). Yes, you have been hurt, marriage shattered, lost job, do not have the money you need, or were abused as a child. Satan may have caused tremendous problems and pain in your life in the past. You may have been an able tool of the devil, but your past is now past. The problem today is not so much with your past but with your reactions and responses to you past. Your reactions and responses may become STRONGHOLDS that you voluntarily hide behind to protect yourself from further pain. (Never get close to anyone again; never love with your whole heart; never try as hard; never trust anyone, etc.,.) Fear of the past can lead you to make wrong choices in the present.

Wrong choices may slow down your progress, but if you repent and allow the Holy Spirit to teach you, you will be placed back on track and start moving forward again. God can restart you with an unblemished, untarnished, 100 percent, still-intact relationship. The forgiveness, grace and mercy of God will place your past under the blood. You are then free to let go of your past and leave it there. Regardless of what anyone tell you, God's plan and purposes for you are not limited or diminished because you messed up in the past. You are the only one who can limit your ability to receive God's grace. YOU WILL ONLY CHOOSE TO LIMIT THE GRACE OF GOD IN YOUR LIFE if you are HOLIDNG ON TO MENTAL, EMOTIONAL OR SPIRITUAL POLLUTION because of some false concept of God or salvation.

Satan USES our wrong senses, emotions and ideas against us. We hide behind our personally acceptable errors and they become STRONGHOLDS in our lives. We become BOUND to them. Our fears and past pain become doorways that Satan uses to attack and discourage us. We have held on to many positions and ideas from the past in our feeble effort to protect ourselves. We have believed the lie that we are UNLOVED, UNWANTED, UNCECESSARY, UNSUCCESSFUL, UNWORHTY, SPIRITUALLY AND EMOTIONALLY UGLY. If in our hearts we believe these lies to be true, we will build a STRONGHOLD around them to protect them. We will become SUSPICIOUS of anyone trying to convince us that we have believed a lie. We even become suspicious of God and

the truths of the Bible.

Building STRONGHOLDS is like putting yourself against the other side of a wall that you have built, not letting anyone over, or letting yourself out. You think you're protecting yourself, but you're not, you are causing more damage than good. If you have built STRONGHOLDS around the painful issues of your life, Satan will use them to keep you away from continuing your PROCESS of Spiritual Growth. Satan knows about your unmet needs, unresolved memories, pain, anger, bitterness, unforgiveness, resentment, fears and hidden sin. He will use these burdens to attack you.

Rom. 10:4-13. This NEW BIRTH is a PROCESS. Satan also knows about the process, therefore he will attempt to get you to stop the process. When you surrender to Jesus you receive a new identity. You are FORGIVEN, SAVED, and walking with God. Satan moves quickly and often quietly to CHIP AWAY at your new identity. He attacks through the pulls of our flesh, feelings and focus of life. As new believers, we are still in the flesh with "technical" new natures that are still being WORKED OUT and WORKED INTO our minds. The real trouble starts as we begin to grow spiritually. Part of process is becoming LOOSED from Satan, his bondage and our personal hurts, pains and areas of non-forgiveness, which have now become new STRONGHOLDS.

In order to respond properly to your circumstances, your mind, will, and emotions must be BOUND to the will of God, and LOOSED FROM your wrong senses and emotions. With the RIGHT KEY, you can LOCK yourself to Christ and UNLOCK yourself from your past. This will allow you to SUBMIT to His will and make the right choices.

The ROOT PROBLEM is your DAMAGED HEART and the STRONGHOLDS you have built to protect it. Your barriers sometimes keep the pain out, but mostly they KEEP THE PAIN IN. THE QUEST ION IS not do you have problems, but what are you going to do about them? God is not your problem. Your OLD NATURE is

your problem. BINDING and LOOSING makes it possible to CRUCIFY that old nature and receive God's full healing and restoration. Matt. 16:19; 18:18.

God does not want to keep any good thing from you. The devil cannot keep any good thing from you. Only you can OPPOSE your receiving what God has in store for you. **You can STOP OPPOSING YOURSELF by stripping off, tearing down and moving out of the STRONGHOLDS of your old nature THEREBY ENLARGING YOU CAPACITY TO RECEIVE.**

RESTORATION TAKES TIME

PART THREE

KEY TEXT: EPH 4:24, 25

Satan USES our wrong senses, emotions and ideas against us. We hide behind our personally acceptable errors and they become STRONGHOLDS in our lives. We become BOUND to them. Our fears and past pain become doorways that Satan uses to attack and discourage us. We have held on to many positions and ideas from the past in our feeble effort to protect ourselves. We have believed the lie that we are UNLOVED, UNWANTED, UNCECESSARY, UNSUCCESSFUL, UNWORHTY, SPIRITUALLY AND EMOTIONALLY UGLY. If in our hearts we believe these lies to be true, we will build a STRONGHOLD around them to protect them. We will become SUSPICIOUS of anyone trying to convince us that we have believed a lie. We even become suspicious of God and the truths of the Bible.

If you have built STRONGHOLDS around the painful issues of your life, Satan will use them to keep you away from continuing your PROCESS of Spiritual Growth. Satan knows about your unmet needs, unresolved memories, pain, anger, bitterness, unforgiveness, resentment, fears and hidden sin. He will use these burdens to attack you.

Rom. 10:4-13. This NEW BIRTH is a PROCESS. Satan also knows about the process, therefore he will attempt to get you to stop the process. When you surrender to Jesus you receive a new identity. You are FORGIVEN, SAVED, and walking with God. We've learned that Satan moves quickly and often quietly to CHIP AWAY at your new identity. He attacks through the pulls of our flesh, feelings and focus of life. As new believers, we are still in the flesh with "technical" new natures that are still being WORKED OUT and WORKED INTO our minds. The real trouble starts as we begin to grow spiritually. Part of process is becoming LOOSED from Satan, his bondage and our personal hurts, pains and areas of non-forgiveness, which have now become new STRONGHOLDS.

In order to respond properly to your circumstances, your mind, will and emotions must be BOUND to the will of God and LOOSED FROM your wrong senses and emotions. With the RIGHT KEY you can LOCK yourself to Christ and UNLOCK yourself from your past. This will allow you to SUBMIT to His will and make the right choices.

The ROOT PROBLEM is your DAMAGED HEART and the STRONG-HOLDS you have built to protect it. Your barriers sometimes keep the pain out, but mostly they KEEP THE PAIN IN. THE QUESTION IS not do you have problems, but what are you going to do about them? God is not your problem. Your OLD NATURE is your problem. BINDING and LOOSING makes it possible to CRUCIFY that old nature and receive God's full healing and restoration. Matt. 16: 19; 18:18.

God does not want to keep any good thing from you. The devil cannot keep any good thing from you. Only YOU can OPPOSE receiving what God has in store for you. You can STOP OPPOSING YOURSELF by stripping off, tearing down and moving out of the STRONGHOLDS of your old nature THEREBY ENLARGING YOU CAPACITY TO RECEIVE.

OUR STRONGHOLDS leave open far too many doors of access for the enemy to work. Most Christians are prepared for a FRONTAL attack. We see the enemy coming and we take our stand. The enemies will flee, however, Satan does not always come at us directly. He often approaches the open doors and back windows of our spiritual house. We stand ready at the front door, so he enters the back. James 4:7. (where does Satan go AFTER he flees from us?) He searches for signs of BITTERNESS (stronghold), UNFORGIVENESS (stronghold) PRIDE (stronghold) UNBELIEF (stronghold).

God in His mercy is always working to help us overcome our strongholds. However, He will not overlook or excuse the sin practiced as a result of the strongholds in your life. God will not allow you to hang onto NEGATIVE feelings and BITTERNESS and still enter into the FULLNESS of your inheritance. 1 Peter. 3:12. The word "EVIL" here carries the meaning of a bad nature; not such as it ought to be; a MODE of thinking, feeling or acting that is base, wrong or wicked. God works against those who are not in right standing with Him. He does not allow them to enter into the FULLNESS of their inheritance until they have settled the stronghold issues. (see book of Job)

God in His mercy has spared many of us while we operated in UNBELIEF, REBELLION and DISOBEDIENCE. We were DISOBEDIENT when the Holy Spirit convicted us of God's plea to tear the stronghold down, and we ignored that plea. *This is not about merely LOVING the Lord, but rather letting that LOVE direct you to obey God and cooperate with His directions.*
2 Corinthians. 5:18,19. The word RECONCILIATION in these verses means exchange or restoration to favor with God. Part of this RESTORATION occurs as we are TRANSFORMED by the RENEWING and RENOVATION of our minds. (Rom. 12:2) Renovation and renewal imply a MAJOR clean-up and construction project. The stinky, stained old things in your mind, will, and emotions have to be shoveled out, torn up, stripped away, broken apart and removed to make room for your renewed self. 2 Kings 4:1-7; Mal. 4: 5,6; Joel 2:25-32. We partake of this restoration by making room to receive it. We receive it by using the keys of surrender and change.

THE POWER OF BINDING AND LOOSING

KEY TEXT: JOHN 15:3-5

Hell is only able to sustain its program against you if it is not RESISTED. It is difficult to RESIST when you are divided against yourself and opposing yourself. You oppose yourself when the things you believe about yourself have more control of your life than the word of God. You oppose yourself when what you believe about your past has more influence upon you than what God says about your future.

There is a BINDING that relates more to imprisonment and chains. There is also a BINDING that relates more to joining together, knitting together and tying up. The central idea of captivity remains present with both ideas, although one emphasizes the more positive aspects and the other more negatives. Proverbs. 3:1-6; Proverbs. 6:20-23.

Many people see only the side of BINDING that connects to the act of CHAINING SOMETHING UP so it can no longer hurt them. There is also the POSITIVE BINDING such as BINDING a baby to the body of its mother. As children of God we can BIND OURSELVES to the STEADFAST things of God. We can BIND our days and nights to the will of God, all in the name of Jesus. As we BIND ourselves to the life of the FATHER, He can keep us balanced and sure-footed in our spiritual walk. The FATHER can easily pass through the narrowest, most dangerous pathways. He can LEAD US through the valley, even the valley containing death. Matt. 6:9,10.

We can BIND OURSELVES to the truth of God. This BINDING will (John 15:3-5) give us a new SENSE OF AWARENESS of our own thoughts, and patterns of weakness in our lives. We then become SENSATIVE to spiritual insights that come from the Holy Spirit. We begin to SENSE the hidden agendas, unseen feelings, motivations, past hurts and pains that lead to senseless behavior. We will become more sensitive to the underlying issues and not spend our time reacting to the WORDS and the WALLS people throw at us or we throw at ourselves. Sometimes we experience painful events, cruel words and times of rejection and our reaction to these incidents get played back in our minds constantly. As we REHEARSE our HURTS we rewrite the situations with sharp words and putdowns that we wished we had said. As we are BOUND to these situations in our minds, these words and attitudes SLIP OUT at the first sign of provocation. As soon as we are under pressure we exhibit those things we have become BOUND TO. It doesn't automatically stop when we become Christians. With our new understanding of Binding and Loosing, we can use the same technique to change our attitudes and outlooks on life.

We can BIND OURSELVES to the mind of Christ. II Cor. 10: 3-5. You will begin to recognize when your thoughts have slipped out of line. You will also realize that you can CHOOSE to think other thoughts.   Making the choice may be hard, very hard for some, yet the CONSTANT binding of your mind to the will of God will strengthen you for consistent victory. PS.91:1-7.

We can BIND OURSELVES to the blood of Jesus. The blood can cleanse our consciences from dead works. We can BIND OURSELVES to an awareness of its healing power, protection, covering and cleansing.

There is POWER IN THE TONGUE. There is POWER IN THE WORD. If we would use the WORD already blessed by God to this work of BINDING and LOOSING, we will begin to see the deeper problem areas where we need deliverance i.e.:

- UNFORGIVENESS
- LUST
- RESENTMENT

WE ARE IN A BATTLE AGAINST

DEMOMC FORCES

We need DELIVERANCE and SPIRITUAL DEVELOPMENT in FIVE areas.

(1) DELIVERANCE from SIN into SALVATION.
- a. Are you SAVED? What does it mean to be SAVED?
- b. Justification (salvation <u>PROVIDED FOR YOU</u>)
- c. Sanctification (salvation <u>DEMONSTRATED IN YOU</u>)

(2) DELIVERANCE from DEMONIC oppression and INFLUENCE

(3) BAPTISM a public expression of 1 & 2.

(4) DISCIPLING PROCESS
- d. You are TAUGHT and TRAINED to walk in the LIGHT
- e. provided by 1, 2 and 3.
- f. You receive and begin to operate within the context of your Spiritual gifts.

(5) REVIVAL when we have failed or slacked off in any of the above

The Greek noun for *DEMON* gives rise to a verb in connection to the word demon. The English equivalent of this verb is *DEMONISE* which is defined as being "subject to demonic influence." In the New Testament this verb means, "to be demonized." In the original KJV this verb is regularly translated as "to be possessed of or with a devil or devils." Most modern versions have correctly changed the word *DEVIL* to *DEMON,* but incorrectly retain the form *to be possessed.*

The problem is that with our English ears, the word *POSSESS* suggests to us OWNERSHIP rather than being subject to demonic influence. Every born-again Christian sincerely seeking to live for Christ BELONGS to Christ and is OWNED BY HIM. That person does not belong to the devil nor is owned by the devil. ON THE OTHER HAND, a born-again Christian can be subject to demonic influences. Such a Christian undoubtedly belong to Christ, yet there are areas of his or her life that have not yet come under the control of the Holy Spirit. There is still the foundation and influence of the OLD NATURE. It is these areas that may still be subject to demonic influence. In order to experience complete freedom and release in these areas, it may be necessary for the demonic forces to be EXPELLED.

Satan has developed a special opposition to the ministry of EXPELLING those demons that are influencing the children of God. This area of ministry is largely ignored by many churches. Evangelism in the West has frequently been practiced as if demons do not exist. How can we pray for people as the Bible requires and yet fail to EXPEL demons that the same Bible commands us to EXPEL.

There are those who carry the practice of casting out demons to unscriptural extremes. They give God and ministry a bad name. They give the impression that any kind of problem - physical, emotional or spiritual -should be treated as demonic. This is unbalanced and unscriptural. Sometimes deliverance is carried out in a way that places the spotlight on the ministry or on the one receiving deliverance than on the Lord Jesus. Many are afraid to even speak of EXPELLING demons or discussing the topic. One author said, "the fear of demons is from the demons themselves."

Mark 1:21-28. How did Jesus practice DELIVERANCE MINISTRY? Notice that His emphasis was on TEACHING THE WORD with AUTHORITY. It was during this time of teaching ministry that the man with the evil spirit began to cry out. Vs. 23-NKJV says *WITH* an UNCLEAN Spirit. The Greek actually says *IN AN* unclean spirit. Perhaps the nearest English equivalent would be *under the* INFLUENCE *of an unclean spirit*. The NIV translates this phrase as *POSSESSED by an evil* spirit. This translation obscures the meaning of the text. It gives the suggestion of ownership.

The man's MIND had been darkened by demonic forces, but when he came into the presence of Jesus, a ray of light pierced the darkness, and he cried out for help. He wanted freedom but the demon resisted the power of Christ. "When the man tried to appeal to Jesus for help, the evil spirit PUT WORDS INTO HIS MOUTH, and he cried out in an agony of fear. The demoniac PARTIALLY COMPREHENDED that he was in the presence of ONE who could set him free, but when he tried to come within reach of that mighty hand, ANOTHER'S WILL HELD HIM, another's WORDS found utterance through him." Desire of Ages 214.

The SAME EVIL SPIRIT that tempted Christ in the wilderness AND THAT POSSESSED THE MANIAC, also CONTROLLED THE UNBELIEVING JEWS. But with them he ASSUMED an AIR OF PIETY, seeking to deceive them AS TO their MOTIVES in rejecting Jesus. Their condition was *more hopeless than that of the demoniac,* for they felt no need of Christ and were therefore held fast under the power of Satan. <u>The period of Christ's personal ministry among men WAS THE TIME of the greatest activity for the forces of the kingdom of darkness.</u> As Jesus was revealing to men the true character of God and breaking Satan's power, the demonic forces were becoming more active. New life and power was coming down from above, and the prince of evil was rallying all of his forces to fight against the kingdom of God every step of the way.

The battle will be fought in the same manner in the last days. New life and power will descend from on high from God and new life and power will spring up from beneath energizing the workers of Satan. 1 Tim. 4:1 <u>Side by side, with the preaching of the gospel, demons are at work with lying spirits. Secret sins are not surrendered to God. Passion, hatred and unforgiveness grip our hearts. Satan is delighted, and we are weakened and discouraged.</u>

There is still hope. John 8:32; 7: 17. No one has fallen so low nor become so vile that Christ cannot save him or her. The demonized man tried to pray, but only the demon's words came out. Yet Jesus heard what the man's mouth could not say. Jesus heard his heart cry. Jesus still hears every heart's cry. Isaiah. 27:5, 49:24,25.

Mark 1:23-34. Please note that people came to Jesus seeking healing but many of them had demons cast out of them. Apparently the people did not realize that some of their sicknesses were caused by demons. What kind of people was Jesus ministering to in this way? Primarily observant Jews, who met every Sabbath in the synagogue, and spent the rest of the week caring for their families and minding their business. The people who received help from Jesus were mainly normal, respectable, religious people. Yet they were demonized. A demon had gained access to some area or areas of their lives and as a result they were not in full control.

There are many similar people to be found in the Christian community who are good, respectable, religious church attendees who are just like the Jews of Jesus' day. Some have areas in their lives that have been invaded by demons and as a result, they are not in full control. Matthew 10:1, 7, 8.

WE WRESTLE NOT AGAINST

FLESH AND BLOOD

KEY TEXT: EPH 6: 12

DEMONS are spiritual enemies and it is the responsibility of each Christian to deal with them directly in spiritual warfare. Demon spirits can invade and indwell human bodies. It is their objective to do so. By indwelling a person they obtain a greater advantage in controlling that person than when they are working from the outside. When demons indwell a person that person is said to have evil spirits or to be possessed with demons. The word translated "possessed" by the KJV should be translated "demonized" or "have demons." Much misunderstanding has resulted from the used of the word "possessed." This word suggests TOTAL OWNERSHIP. In this sense a Christian could never be "demon possessed". He could not be OWNED by demons, because he or she is owned by Christ.

1 Pet. 1:18,19; & 1 Corinthians. 6:19,20. Indwelling demons are unnecessary and undesirable TRESPASSERS. Trespassers are those who UNLAWFULY and STEALTHILY encroach upon the territory of another. Trespassers can continue their UNLAWFUL practices UNTIL they are confronted and challenged on the basis of LEGAL RIGHTS. Since Jesus Christ has purchased us with His own blood, we belong to Him. The devil has no LEGAL right to us. Therefore no demon can remain when the Christian seriously desires him to go. James 4:7.

Demons consider the body of the person to be their house. Matt 12:43,44. Twenty-five times in the New Testament, demons are called "unclean spirits." The word unclean is the same word used to designate certain creatures which the Israelites were not to eat. Acts 10:11-14. Not only were the animals literal creatures, unfit for consumption, they also served as spiritual examples of incorrect behavior. As a spiritual example, the pig (unclean) is to the natural realm what the demon (unclean) is to the spiritual realm. Just as the Israelite zealously protected themselves from contact with pigs, the Christian is to guard himself from the contact with evil spirits.

All four Gospels, record the event of Jesus CLEANSING THE TEMPLE. (Please note that your body is the TEMPLE of the Holy Ghost). This CLEANSING of the temple gives us an unusual picture of Jesus. Mark 11:15-19. Jesus began personally and determinedly to PURGE the temple of every DEFILING THING. This is an illustration of the cleansing of our bodies, which are the TEMPLE of the Holy Spirit. Demons provide nothing good, they only defile. Jesus did not make any pretty little speeches or debate with those who defiled the temple - He DROVE THEM OUT.

The amazing thing is, some Christians are not as quick to get rid of indwelling demons as one might assume. Some are embarrassed to admit the need for deliverance. (The embarrassment should not come from having them, but in failing to act in getting them out). Some have walked in agreement with certain spirits for so long that they do not want to change. Not all Christians really want to live in purity. Some have made friends with pigs. But even the prodigal son came to *himself* WHILE AMONG THE PIGS and decided that he would SEPARATE HIMSELF and return to his father.

Eph. 6:10-12; II Corinthians. 10:3,4. Wrestling speaks of close-quarter fighting, of personally grappling with the powers of darkness. Most of us would prefer to use a long-range shotgun and blast away at these enemies from miles away, but this is not possible. The battle is very personal, and close. This enemy is a spiritual one. The weapons used to defeat this enemy are spiritual. Wrestling suggest BALANCE and PRESSURE tactics. Satan will put PRESSURE on us and throw us OFF BALANCE. He does this in our thought life, emotions, decision-making and our physical bodies. In order to win in this battle, the Christian must throw away the ineffective fleshly weapons and take up spiritual weapons.

FIRST we are fighting against PRINCIPALITIES. This word is used to describe things in a series, as leaders, rulers and magistrates. Thus a "series" of leaders or rulers would describe this rank and organization. "Principalities" tell us that Satan's army is highly organized. Satan is the head and under him are ruling spirits who are in submission to him. These ruling spirits are assigned over areas such as nations, cities and churches. (Daniel 10:10-14). The "prince of Persia" was a demon prince. Problems that PERSIST and PLAGUE churches and homes may indicate that special evil agents have been assigned to cause trouble in these areas.

SECOND, we warfare against POWERS. POWERS is accurately translated as "authorities." Demons are placed over various areas or territories and are given authority to carry out whatever orders they have been given. The Christian has also been given greater authority to deal with the authority of the demons. Mark 16:17. Demons are forced to yield to the authority of the name of Jesus. The demons also have POWER. The Christian also has POWER. Acts 1:8, Luke 9:1 & 10:17-19. The POWER of the believer comes with the baptism of the Holy Spirit. The AUTHORITY comes through SALVATION. These gifts of POWER and AUTHORITY are SUPERNATURAL. They are given to believers to overcome demon powers. We are not to wait for God to give us this power. He has ALREADY PROVIDED for our salvation and our baptism in the Holy Spirit. God is waiting for us to RECOGNIZE that He has already made provision for our victory in war. (Policeman have both authority and power)

THIRD, we wrestle with THE RULERS OF DARKNESS OF THIS WORLD. These are the Lords of this world or Princes of this age. Lords and Princes love to CONTROL. Jesus is able to override their control and trespassing. Luke 11:20-22.

FOURTH we wrestle against SPIRITUAL WICKEDNESS in HIGH PLACES. The key to this phrase is the word WICKEDNESS. These evil powers have only one objective - WICKEDNESS. They may appear as angels of light and by their deceptions draw many into their nets of destruction. When we fail to become involved in spiritual warfare we show that we do not care what becomes of ourselves, our families, our community, our church, our nation and world.

Part two of this study deals with how Jesus dealt with this subject. What was his method? How did he apply it?

WHAT ARE SOME OF THE CLUES INDICATING POSSIBLE DEMONIC PRESENCE?

The best words to use are **afflicted**, **in bondage**, **oppressed**, **demonized**, or **tormented**. The most common word nowadays is demonized, and it denotes that there is a presence there but certainly not possession for the Christian. It is more like a demon ATTACHES itself to something, such as a recurring bad habit or sin practice and has reason to be there.

WHO IS IN CONTROL? Is the person totally in control or does the phrase continually repeat. "I have prayed and confessed and cried but I cannot get the victory over this besetting sin." When praying, crying and confessing are not quite enough, it is a pretty good clue that perhaps a demonic presence is involved. The person does not control that problem, but that problem controls them.

A FEELING OF TOTAL HELPLESSNESS OVER AN EMOTION OR SITUATION. A feeling of hopelessness also sets in. It could be something like hatred toward a person who wronged you and whenever the thought comes to mind or you see a picture of that person, the emotion boils up once again. Even after confessing it to the Lord, it just won't go away permanently.

SOMETHING CAME OVER ME. A person can be in one frame of mind one moment and then, like the sudden switch of a light, darkness overtakes the person. A totally different frame of mind kicks in and the person gets out of control in some emotional or behavioral area.

A VOICE TOLD ME TO DO SOMETHING TERRIBLE. Experts say that some mental illnesses can be accompanied by voices that are not necessarily demonic in nature. But when the voice tells the person to do something clearly sinful, evil or deadly one should certainly investigate the possibility of demonic activity.

PAST INVOLVEMENT IN WITCHCRAFT, SATANISM, FREEMASONRY AND OTHER SECRET SOCITEIES that take unholy vows, engage in the worship of any deity other than Jehovah God and His Son Jesus Christ, or make use of magic, curses or spells to affect, control or harm others. Unholy vows and covenants are made that are demonic in nature and provide openings for curses. These activities are open invitations to demons. These curses and activities must be renounced and broken in the **name of Jesus**. Demons can be evicted.

In deliverance we always work backward, asking the questions, "what seems to be the problem and when did t first start?" Why? Because most demons have been around for a very long time. One must get to the root in order for deliverance to take place.

There are the negative influences of certain movies, music and TV programs. Exposure to so much violence and improper sexual images lead to callousness and confusion. The concept of what is evil is watered down. This leaves open the door to inviting demons into our lives because we do not know any better.

Many churches do not believe in the supernatural. They do not believe in miracles, praying for the sick, laying on of hands or casting out demons. There is skimpy teaching on tithing, forgiveness, honesty and especially holiness. People are rushed into baptism without fully understanding the decision they have made. There are many walking around wounded in the church. Some churches develop counseling ministries designed to comfort the afflicted rather than adopting more radical measures for them. Unfortunately some Pastors and leaders with demonic bondage have no help. There is just no one to turn to when leaders themselves need deliverance. Satanism, witchcraft and Freemasonry are alive and well and operative in our communities and even in our churches. Many are unaware that witches and Satanist have been given specific assignments against some Pastors and churches. Most do not have the prayer protection or spiritual warfare tools to do effective combat.

WHEN IS DELIVERANCE NEEDED?

KEY TEXT: PSALM 18:1, 2

DELIVERANCE means *"to set free or liberate: as in, they were delivered from bondage."* Much of the general ministry of deliverance can be learned. With experience, and the help from the Holy Spirit, it is a valuable ministry. Some are more gifted than others, but it is hard to get away from the fact that Jesus told His followers to do it. Every Christian should have the basic ability to cast out a demon. Even the disciples got to see Jesus do it, and to apprentice with Him for years. Luke 9:1; Acts 1:8. They were instructed that there are different kinds of demons and some can only come out by fasting and prayer.

Casting out demons has gained a bad reputation in many churches and denominations, because of misunderstanding and abuse. Many people have misgivings because they were prayed over and "it didn't work." People are often in far too much of a hurry to cast out a demon without knowing why it is there or dealing with the entry points. In the attempt to cure a symptom, they neglect the cause. The person may have temporary relief, but before long, if the ENTRY POINT has not been healed, the demon returns again and may bring along some friends. Healing and closing the entry points are the only way that true deliverance can take place. (Entry points are clearly defined in the previous chapter, and will be further explained under 'A' in this chapter).

Another misunderstanding arises from the fact that we are dealing with the *INVISIBLE WORLD.* People don't like to mess with something they don't understand and cannot see. Some people are gifted in **discernment,** while others are more gifted in **deduction,** others just don't want to mess with a demon period.

WE NEED DELIVERANCE BECAUSE:

A. A 70% divorce rate has torn homes apart and moms have to work and struggle to make ends meet. Kids are often alone and have TV as their teacher or abusive neighbors and family members as their guardians. Instability, insecurity and uncertainty are part of our modern lives. Many kids can't understand the concept of a loving heavenly Father because they have never seen a loving earthy father. Demonic entry points can include rejection, unforgiveness, abandonment and many others.

B. There is a level of tolerance for evil, whether it is right or wrong, the worst thing one can do nowadays is be intolerant. This has been a factor in advancing the homosexual agenda. People are all mixed up because they confuse love for the sinner, with tolerance. We are taught that it's okay to do almost anything, and as a result, experimentation opens doors to demons of lust, addiction, violence and other perverse things. Sexual demons are taking advantage of easy openings. Remember we are to love the sinner BUT HATE THE SIN. SIN IS NEVER RIGHT OR APPROPRIATE.

C. There are the negative influences of certain movies, music and TV programs. Exposure to so much violence and improper sexual images lead to callousness and confusion. The concept of what is evil is watered down. This leaves open the door to inviting demons into our lives because WE DO NOT KNOW ANY BETTER.

D. Many churches do not believe in the supernatural. They do not believe in miracles, praying for the sick, laying on of hands or casting out demons. They talk about these things, read them and may even preach about them, but do not believe in them, nor in the power to do them, probably because of fear of the unknown. There is skimpy teaching on tithing, forgiveness, honesty and especially holiness. People are rushed into baptism without fully understanding the decision they have made, and the war they have now enrolled in.

E. There are many walking around wounded in the church. Some churches develop counseling ministries designed to comfort the afflicted rather than adopting more radical measures for them. Unfortunately some Pastors and leaders with demonic bondage have no help. There is just no one to turn to when leaders themselves need deliverance. Satanism, witchcraft and Freemasonry are alive and well and operative in our communities and even in our churches. Many are unaware that witches and Satanist have been given specific assignments against some Pastors and churches. Jude 4 clearly states that there are ungodly men sent by the devil to oppress the church. Most do not have the prayer protection or spiritual warfare tools to do effective combat.

WHAT ARE SOME OF THE CLUES INDICATING POSSIBLE DEMONIC PRESENCE?

The words to use to describe demonic presence are afflicted, in bondage, oppressed, demonized, tormented, or demonized. Demonized denotes that there is a presence there but certainly not possession for the Christian. It is more like a demon ATTACHES itself to something, such as a recurring bad habit or sin practice and because of this, it has reason to be there.

WHO IS IN CONTROL? Is the person totally in control or does the phrase continually repeat, "I have prayed and confessed and cried but I cannot get the victory over this sin." When praying, crying and confessing are not quite enough, it is a pretty good clue that perhaps a demonic presence is involved. The person does not control that problem, but that problem controls them.

A FEELING OF TOTAL HELPLESSNESS OVER AN EMOTION OR SITUATION. A feeling of hopelessness also sets in. It could be something like hatred toward a person who wronged you and whenever the thought comes to mind or you see a picture of that person, the emotion boils up once again. Even after confessing it to the Lord, it just won't go away permanently. 1 Corinthians 10:13 says "God will always make a way of escape." The only time we see helplessness in scripture is in a demonic behavior. Matthew 12:22

SOMETHING CAME OVER ME. A person can be in one frame of mind one moment and then, like the sudden switch of a light, darkness overtakes the person. A totally different frame of mind kicks in and the person gets out of control in some emotional or behavioral area. Whenever someone gets out of control it is the prince of darkness. The only time we see people out of control in the bible is when they are controlled by devils. Mark 5: 1-21

A VOICE TOLD ME TO DO SOMETHING TERRIBLE. Experts say that some mental illnesses can be accompanied by voices that are not necessarily demonic in nature. But when the voice tells the person to do something clearly sinful, evil or deadly one should certainly investigate the possibility of demonic activity.

PAST INVOLVEMENT IN WITCHCRAFT, SATANISM, FREEMASONRY AND OTHER SECRET SOCITEIES that take unholy vows, engage in the worship of any deity other than Jehovah God and His Son Jesus Christ, or make use of magic, curses or spells to affect, control or harm others. Unholy vows and covenants are made that are demonic in nature and provide openings for curses. These activities are open invitations to demons. These curses and activities must be renounced and broken in the name of Jesus. Demons can be evicted. Mark 5:12,13.

In deliverance we always work backward, asking the questions, "what seems to be the problem, and when did it first start?" Why? Because most demons have been around for a very long time. One must get to the root in order for deliverance to take place. If any of the above consistently occurs, seek help, don't let the devil have control of your life, you need deliverance.9

Seven Steps to Deliverance

1. Honesty

One must be honest with himself and with God if he expects to receive God's blessing of deliverance. Lack of honesty keeps areas of one's life in darkness. Demon spirits thrive on such darkness. Honesty helps bring them into the light. Any sin not confessed or repented, gives the demon a "legal right" to remain. Ask God to help you see yourself as He sees you, and to bring to light anything that is not of Him.

I acknowledge my sin unto thee, and mine iniquity have I not hid. I said, I will confess my transgressions unto the Lord; and thou forgave the iniquity of my sin. Psalm 32:5

Search me, O God, and know my heart: try me, and know my thoughts: and see if there be any wicked way in me, and lead me in the way everlasting. Psalm 139:23,24

2. Humility

This involves recognition that one is dependent upon God and His provisions for deliverance.

God resisteth the proud, but giveth grace unto the humble. Submit yourselves therefore to God. Resist the devil and he will flee from you. James 4:6,7

It also involves a complete openness with God's servants ministering in the deliverance.

Confess your faults one to another and pray one for another, that he may be healed. James 5:16

3. Repentance

Repentance is a determined turning away from sin and Satan. One must hate all evil in his life and fall out of agreement with it.

"Can two walk together, Except they be agreed?" (Amos 3:3) One must loathe his sins.

> *And there shall remember your ways, and all your doings wherein ye have been defiled: and ye shall loathe yourselves in your own sight for all that ye have your evils committed. Ezekiel 20:43*

Deliverance is not to be used merely to gain relief from problems but in order to become more like Jesus through obedience to all God requires. Repentance is a turning from all that hinders spiritual growth, ministry and fellowship. Repentance requires open confession of all sin. It takes away the legal right of demon spirits.

4. Renunciation

Renunciation is the forsaking of evil. Renunciation is action resulting from repentance.

> *When he (John the Baptist) saw many of the Pharisees and Sadducees come to his baptism, he said unto them, o generation of vipers, who hath warned you to flee from the wrath to come?" Bring Forth Fruits therefore Meet for Repentance.*
> *Matt. 3:7,8*

Bringing forth fruits meet for repentance involves more than words. It is a demonstration of repentance... evidence that one has truly turned from his sins. For example, if one repents of lust he may need to destroy some pornographic materials. If one has repented of religious error he may need to completely renounce it by destroying all literature and items associated with that error.

And many that believed came, and confessed, and hewed their deeds. Many of them also which used curious arts brought their books together and burned them before all men; and they counted the price of them, and found it fifty thousand pieces of silver. Acts 19:18,19

Renunciation means a clean break with Satan and all his works.

5. Forgiveness

God freely forgives all who confess their sins and ask forgiveness through His Son. (See: 1 John 1:9) <u>He expects us to forgive all others who have ever wronged us in any way.</u>

> *For if ye forgive men their trespasses, your heavenly Father will also forgive you: But if ye forgive not men their trespasses, neither will your Father forgive your trespasses. Matt. 6:14,15*

Willingness to forgive is absolutely essential to deliverance. (See: Matt. 18:21-35). No deliverance minister can effect deliverance unless the candidate has met God's conditions.

6. Prayer

Ask God to deliver you and set you free in the name of Jesus.

> *Whosoever shall call upon the name of the Lord shall be delivered. Joel 2:32*

7. Warfare

Prayer and warfare are two separate and distinct activities. Prayer is toward God and warfare is toward the enemy. Our warfare against demon powers is not fleshly but spiritual (See: Eph, 6:19-12;l Corinthians. 10:3-5). Use the weapons of submission to God, the blood of Jesus Christ, the Word of God, and your testimony as a believer. (See: James 4:7; Rev. 12:11; Eph.6: 17). Identify the spirits, address them directly by name in a commanding voice, and in faith command them to go in the name of Jesus. Enter the battle with determination and assurance of victory. Christ cannot fail! He is the Deliverer!

And these signs shall follow them that believe; in my name shall they cast out devils. Mark 16:17

Behold, I give unto you power to tread on serpents and scorpions, and over all the power of the enemy: and nothing shall by any means hurt you. Luke 10:19

The Lord is my rock, and my fortress, and MY DELIVERER. Psalm 18:2

YOU ARE NOW FREE INDEED

KEY TEXT: JOHN 8:32-36

While it is an effective act of Spiritual Warfare to BIND the devil, that is not the only thing necessary in the battle against evil. BINDING evil spirits can deactivate their power, which takes care of the FRONTAL ATTACKS. Still needed are a closing of DOORS, destruction of BRIDGES, healing of WOUNDS and detachment from RESENTMENTS. If all we do is command Satan to leave, without taking the necessary steps to keep him out, nothing much will change. If all we do is command him to leave, without closing the doors and windows through which he came, we will eventually be right back in the same place.

All problems are not caused by the devil or his agents. There are THREE kinds of SPIRITS we have to deal with. (1) The Holy spirit (2) evil spirits and (3) Human spirits. There are some things that are initiated by the Holy Spirit, some by evil spirits and some things happen because of a twisted human character. Too often believers BLAME everything wrong on Satan or an evil angel. Because most of us are lacking in spiritual discernment we DENY and OVERLOOK our own culpability in creating discord and distress. Believers can be the cause of many of their problems. Many times they are solely responsibility. We can manifest some of the ugliest personalities and characters. Satan is happy when he gets the blame for something we have done. The misplaced blame allows us to continue in our foolishness.

1. Evil spirits do exist and they work through people. They need to be bound. We need to be delivered. But after deliverance, then what? You will still find yourself having to eventually deal with the doorway or bridge problem that allows such destructive behavior. You can spend all of your

time fighting the devil or resisting the devil by blocking his access to your life.

2.   What is it that Satan uses to keep believers in turmoil? He uses our STRONGHOLDS. Remember, your strongholds are YOUR personally designed means of protecting yourself AFTER THE NEED FOR PROTECTION HAS PASSED. Your stronghold _is_ where you hide to keep from dealing with your life and your mistakes and errors. These strongholds are your attitudes, patterns of thinking and beliefs. They keep you spiritually vulnerable to demonic agitation. Some women look for broken men to fix. Some women look for addicted men to abuse them either emotionally or physically. Some men look for unhealthy women to latch on too. Some good men are only attracted to unhealthy women. The sickness within draws sickness from without. Like attacks like. Liars attract liars. People who live on HATE become bonded to people who are full of anger.

There are two types of battles to fight. One against evil and one against ourselves. We have to pick up OUR CROSS AND follow Jesus. The picking up our cross is our PERSONAL battle against us. Let a man deny himself.

There is a STRONG need for deliverance within Christian circles. After the deliverance takes place, one must immediately work on the doorways and areas of access. While Christians cannot be demon POSSESSED, evil spirits can TRESSPASS our spiritual domain. We can give them access to harass and torment us.

If you are prayed up, walking in God's will and filled with the Word and the Holy Spirit, God will guide your words and actions. You may be led to enter into intercession for someone. You may anoint with oil and lay hands on them. You may sense a need for deliverance ministry. If you are BOUND to the will of God and LOOSED from the purposes of the enemy, you will be used to bring your brothers and sisters to victory.

True victory happens only in an atmosphere of love and acceptance. You do not accept the sin, but you love the sinner.

Victory is yours today it's all up to you? Will you continue in sin and bondage be freed today through the blood of JESUS.

Resources & Information

Twelve Steps To Freedom In Christ

Once you make a decision to turn away from sin, there are a number of important things you must do to achieve lasting triumph over temptation and addicting actions.

1. Turn To Jesus!

People struggling with sin may think, "I'll turn to God after I clean up my act, but I'm not good enough to come to Him yet." Here's the plain truth: you can never clean yourself up enough for God – but He will do it for you! Ephesians 2:8-9 tells us, "For it is by grace you have been saved, through faith – and this not from yourselves, it is the gift of God – not by works, so that no one can boast." Jesus loves you and paid for every single one of your sins by His death on the cross.

When you truly repent of your sins and give God your whole life – broken and messy as it may be – He gladly accepts you as His child and gives you a new life. The Bible says, "Put off your old self, which is being corrupted by its deceitful desires; to be made new in the attitude of your minds; and to put on the new self, created to be like God in true righteousness and holiness" (Ephesians 4:22-24).

This describes a new life in God! You take off the old self and are made new by Jesus Christ. You give Him your sinful nature, and He gives you His righteousness and holiness. You give Him your weakness, and He gives you His power.

Simply pray:

"Jesus, I confess that I have sinned again and again. I feel trapped in addicting habits, but I am reaching out to you in hope and faith. Thank You for dying on the cross for me. Please forgive me and grant me a new start today. I give myself to You and invite You to be Lord of my life. Thank you for saving me from the power of sin and death. Please fill me with Your Holy Spirit and give me your power, wisdom and grace so that I can obey You and walk according to Your ways every moment of every day. Amen."

If you prayed the prayer. Please let us know: rayofhope4u@hotmail.com We would like to send you some resources to help you begin your new relationship with God.

In 1 John 1:8-9, God promises to forgive all our sins if we are honest with Him about our failings. Look at King David. The Bible spares no detail about how this great hero of Israel failed miserably when he was tempted sexually (see 2 Samuel 11:1-12:25). When David should have been on the battlefield with his men, he lingered in Jerusalem and happened to see a beautiful woman bathing on her rooftop. Now, that accidental glimpse was not sin. But he allowed his eyes to linger, and that led to lust, which in turn led to adultery, lies, betrayal, and murder.

David fell into the pattern of sin described in James 1:14-15: "But each one is tempted when, by his own evil desire, he is dragged away and enticed. Then, after desire has conceived, it gives birth to sin; and sin, when it is full-grown, gives birth to death."

Yet David found forgiveness and mercy when he finally stopped pretending that nothing was wrong and humbly repented. Read through his heartfelt prayer in Psalm 51, and consider making it your own:

Psalm 51:1-17 For the director of music. A psalm of David. When the prophet Nathan came to him after David had committed adultery with Bathsheba.
Have mercy on me, O God, according to your unfailing love; according to your great compassion blot out my transgressions. Wash away all my iniquity and

cleanse me from my sin. For I know my transgressions, and my sin is always before me. Against you, you only, have I sinned and done what is evil in your sight, so that you are proved right when you speak and justified when you judge. Surely I was sinful at birth, sinful from the time my mother conceived me. Surely you desire truth in the inner parts; you teach me wisdom in the inmost place. Cleanse me with hyssop, and I will be clean; wash me, and I will be whiter than snow. Let me hear joy and gladness; let the bones you have crushed rejoice. Hide your face from my sins and blot out all my iniquity. Create in me a pure heart, O God, and renew a steadfast spirit within me. Do not cast me from your presence or take your Holy Spirit from me. Restore to me the joy of your salvation and grant me a willing spirit, to sustain me. Then I will teach transgressors your ways, and sinners will turn back to you. Save me from bloodguilt, O God, the God who saves me and my tongue will sing of your righteousness. O Lord, open my lips, and my mouth will declare your praise. You do not delight in sacrifice, or I would bring it; you do not take pleasure in burnt offerings. The sacrifices of God are a broken spirit; a broken and contrite heart, O God, you will not despise.

We can also be encouraged by Paul's example. Although he was a great evangelist and wrote much of the New Testament, Paul struggled with something he called "a thorn in the flesh." After pleading with the Lord to remove it, Paul received an answer that gives us hope for any situation or temptation we may face: "But He said to me, 'My grace is sufficient for you, for My power is made perfect in weakness.'" Paul commented, "Therefore I will boast all the more gladly about my weaknesses, so that Christ's power may rest on me" (2 Corinthians 12:9).

Praise God – we are weak, but He is strong! We may fail, but He will give us a new start every time we humbly come to Him!

2. Spend Time With God Daily

It's absolutely essential that we look to God for strength and wisdom each day. Spend time reading, studying and meditating on the Scriptures daily. Start with the passages listed below. The Word of God is your spiritual armor, and you dare not enter the battle without it!

Daily prayer is also necessary for victory. James 1:5-6 instructs us: "If any of you lacks wisdom, he should ask God, who gives generously to all without finding fault, and it will be given to him. But when he asks, he must believe and not doubt, because he who doubts is like a wave of the sea, blown and tossed by the wind."

Learn to cry out to God quickly when confronted by trials, temptation, and a desire to yield to addicting behavior. When Peter was sinking in the waves, he prayed one of the shortest prayers in the Bible – "Lord, save me!" – and was immediately rescued by the Lord (see Matthew 14:22-33).

Prayerfully reflect on the names of God, which reveal His wonderful character, such as Father, Strong Deliverer, Redeemer, Master, Savior, Mighty God, Helper, Light of the World, Faithful and True, Friend of Sinners, the Way, the Truth, and the Life.

Give yourself entirely to God daily. Romans 12:1b-2a says, "Offer your bodies as living sacrifices, holy and pleasing to God – this is your spiritual act of worship. Do not conform any longer to the pattern of this world, but be transformed by the renewing of your mind."

Rest assured: God will deliver you from sinful habits and addicting behavior if you fully trust Him and do not doubt Him or depend on your own thinking. Sometimes this happens instantaneously, but other times He wants us to walk into victory one small step at a time. This walk of faith is described in Proverbs 3:5-8: "Trust in the Lord with all your heart and lean not on your own understanding; in all your ways acknowledge Him, and He will make your paths straight. Do not be wise in your own eyes; fear the Lord and shun evil. This will bring health to your body and nourishment to your bones."

3. Choose Your Allies

Although we certainly must go directly to God, confess our sin, and receive forgiveness, there are times that we really need the Body of Christ. Many who have been freed from pornography say they could not win the battle alone. Consider choosing a trusted ally or two to help you gain the victory over addicting habits. Jesus said, "If two of you on earth agree about anything you ask for, it will be done for you by My Father in heaven. For where two or three come together in My name, there am I with them" (Matthew 18:19-20).

Going to church on Saturday/Sunday morning is great, but honest one-on-one relationships are also very effective. As long as people hide a dark secret, it can have power over them. But when that secret is shared with a trusted counselor, its power can be broken! James 5:16 says, "Therefore confess your sins to each other and pray for each other so that you may be healed. The prayer of a righteous man is powerful and effective."

Of course, it's critically important to find the right person – such as a pastor, counselor, elder, or a very mature Christian friend. It's best if men meet with men and women meet with women. A good mentor demonstrates God's love, mercy and truth while able to ask hard questions, hold a person accountable, and rejoice with each success. Above all, this person must be totally trustworthy and never repeat confidences without a person's permission.

Some people find a great deal of help in overcoming addicting behavior by attending Christian accountability groups that offer confidentiality. Proverbs 11:14b says, "Many advisers make victory sure."

4. Count The Consequences

"Jerry" is a born-again, Spirit-filled Christian who is happily married to a beautiful, caring woman. He's a good dad to his children, a model schoolteacher, well regarded in the community, and a respected leader in his church. Nevertheless, Jerry struggled long and hard with an addiction to porn – even after counseling sessions with his pastor. But one day, his accountability group asked him to look into the future and describe where his addiction to porn would lead. Thoughtfully, he replied, "Ultimately, I would lose my wife, my family, my home, my job, and my ministry." After taking a long, hard look at the consequences, Jerry decided that pornography simply wasn't worth it – and that helped set him free.

Take time to carefully examine your life and think about what is most precious to you. Then ask yourself, Am I really willing to risk it all?

5. Identify Your Triggers

It's important to identify exactly what situations trigger you to stumble and fall into addicting activities – such as walking past a magazine rack at the gas station, driving through a certain part of town, staying in a hotel during a business trip, opening the Sunday paper with the lingerie ads, logging on to the Internet, etc. Once you know your weak points, you must be very methodical about avoiding these situations. For example, if you are tempted to watch pornographic movies on cable TV while away on business trips, ask the hotel to disconnect or remove your television before you enter your room. Another good defense is to call a mentor or accountability partner. That person can agree with you in prayer and speak the truth of God's Word, breaking the power of that temptation.

James 4:7 says, Submit yourselves therefore to God. Resist the devil, and he will flee from you.

If you're married, you may want to enlist your spouse in helping you avoid certain triggers. One man asked his wife to remove all the lingerie sale fliers from the Sunday paper before bringing it into the house. Another man asked his wife to change the password on their computer so he could never log on without her knowledge.

6. "HALT"

The acronym "HALT" may be helpful, reminding you not to get too Hungry, Angry, Lonely, or Tired. Realize that you are more vulnerable to addicting behavior during these times, then HALT – immediately stop what you are doing to pray, read your Bible, and/or call someone for prayer. Of course, you may always call or text +447429721970 for prayer and encouragement.

7. Dig Out The Roots

Another way to gain victory in the future is to examine your past. If you have never forgiven certain people for hurting you, take time to do it right now! Lack of forgiveness hinders the flow of God's power in our lives. Jesus said, "Therefore I tell you, whatever you ask for in prayer, believe that you have received it, and it will be yours. And when you stand praying, if you hold anything against anyone, forgive him, so that your Father in heaven may forgive you your sins" (Mark 11:24-25).

Sometimes, Christians like to move forward without looking back – but if hurts from the past are preventing wholeness today, it may be helpful to deal with these wounds through prayerful Christian counseling. Truth comes through the Spirit of Christ – and as John 8:32 says, "Then you will know the truth, and the truth will set you free." Also, the books listed at the end of this pamphlet are excellent resources for individual study.

8. Take Authority Over Your Eyes

Every Man's Battle, by Arterburn, Stoeker and Yorkey, contains practical hints about how to win over sexual temptation. The authors suggest developing the habit of immediately "bouncing your eyes" away from anything that tempts you. If you're watching a great football game on TV and a sexy beer commercial comes on – zap it with your remote instantly! If you're at work and notice that a co-worker's blouse is too low or her skirt is too high, turn away immediately – or look her squarely in the eyes, and nowhere else. Just as you developed a habit of impure thoughts, you can now develop a habit of purity, with God's help.

9. Grow In God's Word

This teaching is full of powerful Scripture verses to help you grow in spiritual strength and maturity. Take time to look them up and underline them in your Bible, and memorize the ones that are most helpful to you personally. Here are some additional passages to study:

Genesis 39 1	Corinthians 10:12-13
Psalm 51 2	Corinthians 10:3-5
Psalm 119:9-11	Galatians 5:1, 13, 16-18
Proverbs 6:20-24	Ephesians 2:10
Proverbs 23:26-28	Ephesians 5:1-33
Daniel 3	Ephesians 6:10-18
Matthew 26:41	Philippians 4:8
Mark 7:20-23	Colossians 3:1-10
Luke 4:1-12 1	Thessalonians 4:1-8
John 10:10 1	Timothy 6:11-12
John 15:1-17	2 Timothy 2:22
John 17:3	Titus 2:11-14
Acts 15:28-29	1 Peter 2:16
Romans 1:16-32	1 Peter 4:1-6

Romans 6:23   Hebrews 4:15-16

Romans 7:15-8:14   James 1:13-15

Romans 12:1-2   James 4:1-10

Romans 13:12-14   Revelation 2:7

10. Pray Continually

Prayer is our lifeline to the Savior, who can rescue us from every trial, temptation and addiction. The Bible says, "Pray continually" (1 Thessalonians 5:17). You may wish to be guided by this wonderful prayer that Jesus gave His disciples in Matthew 6:9b-13:

"Our Father in heaven, hallowed be Your name." [Spend time praising God for His love, wisdom and power, and for all that He has done for you.]

"Your kingdom come, Your will be done on earth as it is in heaven." [Ask God to fulfill His marvelous purposes in your life, in the lives of your loved ones, and others].

"Give us today our daily bread." [Pray that you will trust Him to give you the strength you need for every situation you may encounter today. Lift up any other needs you or your family may have.]

"Forgive us our debts, as we also have forgiven our debtors." [Confess any sins you have committed and forgive anyone who has sinned against you.]

"And lead us not into temptation, but deliver us from the evil one." [Ask God to help you obey as He leads you away from the road that leads to evil and destruction and guides you in the paths of righteousness. Spend time listening to

His voice speaking in your heart, giving you encouragement, admonition, or instructions. Commit all that you say and do today unto Him.] Amen!

May God bless you as you trust Him each day for strength, wisdom and victory.

11. Get Involved

Why Get Involved in ministry at all?

I feel one of the best ways to grow in our relationship with God, along with worship, Bible study, and relationships with other God-followers, is to get involved in serving Him. In the Bible, James tells us: "Do not merely listen to the word, and so deceive yourselves. Do what it says. Anyone who listens to the word but does not do what it says is like a man who looks at his face in a mirror and, after looking at himself, goes away and immediately forgets what he looks like. But the man who looks intently into the perfect law that gives freedom, and continues to do this, not forgetting what he has heard, but doing it - he will be blessed in what he does." (James 1:22-25)

James understood one big thing about Christians. We love to talk, but we don't necessarily like to get up and out and get it done. It's one thing to proclaim Jesus on Sunday/ Saturday morning. It's quite another to get wrapped up in the lives of others on any given day, for no other reason than to bring a smile to God's face. To maintain freedom you must get involved. Do what the word says...

12. The Anointing breaks the yoke

"20 Command the Israelites to bring you clear oil of pressed olives for the light so that the lamps may be kept burning." (Exodus 27:20) NIV

What is the anointing? The anointing is the very presence of God in our lives. Without the anointing we are powerless and ineffective. In the Old Testament we see many examples of men that were anointed with oil before walking in their call. The Levites were anointed, Saul was anointed before becoming a king;

David also was anointed before becoming King. The anointing is the supernatural power that we all need, not only to be able to walk in the call of our ministry effectively, but also in order to be able to carry out the demands of our Christian live. Jesus was and is our example; He is known as Jesus the Christ; the word Christ means: "The anointed one."

In Exodus 27, we see a few hidden secrets concerning this anointing; we must remember that the Old Testament is the shadow of the reality of the New Testament. In this verse, God is talking to Moses and He establishes a few very important points concerning the anointing:

Every believer is responsible for their own anointing: The anointing can't be delegated. We can't survive out of the anointing of another man; we must pursue that anointing ourselves; we must desire that kind of anointed life. Jesus was more than a miracle worker; Jesus was sinless and perfect. That kind of power is available for each believer. Do you want it?

The anointing is the result of the pressures, pains and tribulations of life: The Bible tells us in this verse: "Command the Israelites to bring you clear oil of hard-pressed olives..." The word press means: "Subject to a lot of pressure and lacking sufficient resources." The anointing will cost you your life; the anointing can't be given to you in seminary or by a big-shot minister laying hands on you in a conference. The anointing comes out of pressure, tribulation, hardship, problems, etc.

We can't be the light of the world if we are not anointed: It is the anointing; that pure oil that produces the light. It is impossible to be the light of the world if we are lacking the anointing of God.

The anointing can't be a one-day or once-in-a-while thing; the anointing must be a daily thing: The Bible tells us here that: "the lamps may be kept burning." This is a typology of the way we ought to go after God and after the power of His anointing. Every day we ought to live powerful lives; that is the example of Christ for the whole world.

Without the anointing we can't learn Spiritual principles: First John 2:27 tells us: "27 But the anointing which you have received from Him abides in you, and you do not need that anyone teach you; but as the same anointing teaches you concerning all things, and is true, and is not a lie, and just as it has taught you, you will abide in Him." NKJV

The word anointing here is the word chrísma, this is where we get the word christós or "Christ" meaning: The Anointed One; it stands for the Holy Spirit.

It is the anointing that destroy the yokes: Isaiah 10:27"It shall come to pass in that day That his burden will be taken away from your shoulder,
And his yoke from your neck,
And the yoke will be destroyed because of the anointing oil." NKJV Only the anointing makes our ministries effective; it is the anointing that make people free.

Talents are irrevocable, but the anointing can be taken away from us due to rebelliousness: 1Samuel 15:23-26

"23 For rebellion is as the sin of witchcraft, And stubbornness is as iniquity and idolatry.
Because you have rejected the word of the Lord, He also has rejected you from being king."

24 Then Saul said to Samuel, "I have sinned, for I have transgressed the commandment of the Lord and your words, because I feared the people and obeyed their voice. 25 Now therefore, please pardon my sin, and return with me, that I may worship the Lord."26 But Samuel said to Saul, "I will not return with you, for you have rejected the word of the Lord, and the Lord has rejected you from being king over Israel." NKJV

Beloved, we need the anointing; it is essential in our Christian lives; it is the power to learn, it is the power to do, the power to say, the power to resist, the power to stay, the power to overcome, the power to leave, the power of restoration, the power to speak, the power to sing, the power to be quiet, the power to confront, the power to overcome, the power to move forward, the power to write, and the power to be all that God has call us to be.

The Most Important Prayer

If you have never asked Jesus to be your Lord and Savior and don't know how, it's easy. It's so simple that many people think it can't be for real . . . but it is! God knew that not one of us would be able to personally make up for the things He doesn't want us to do. This is called sinning or rebelling against God. So He sent His Son Jesus to pay the penalty for the sins of every person once and for all.

For all have sinned and fall short of the glory of God, and are justified freely by his grace through the redemption that came by Christ Jesus. (Rom. 3:23)

While this may be hard for you to understand just now, all you need to do is believe that Jesus died for you, confess to God that there is sin in your life, and accept His forgiveness and His gift of eternal life.

Don't wait another moment, pray this prayer right now and put God in charge of your life:

Dear Lord Jesus, I believe that You are the Son of God. I believe that You died for my sins and rose from the grave. I invite You into my heart and receive You right now. Thank You for forgiveness. Thank You for a new life. Help me to be what You want me to be and live your life through me. Amen.

Have you invited Jesus Christ to be your Lord and Savior? Email me on rayofhope4u@hotmail.com You have just made the most important decision of your life by accepting Jesus Christ as your Lord and Savior. With Him by your side, you are ready to face the road ahead. And you can face it with the assurance of God's promise:

And we know that in all things God works for the good of those who love Him, who have been called according to his purpose. (Rom. 8:28)

YOU ARE NOW FREE INDEED

Typical Symptoms of Possession

These include a lack of energy, weakness in the body, severe depression, disturbed thoughts and/or irrational thinking.
In general a person who is possessed can be identified as being extremely negative and severely depressed and by also exhibiting anti-social behaviour.

Indications of possession include:
• Strong negativity
• Deep depression
• Rapid mood changes
• Uncontrolled temper
• Self inflicted harm
• Violent behaviour
• Criminal behaviour
• Suicidal tendencies
• Chronic illness
• Epilepsy
• Dual (or multiple) personalities

Even one or two of these indicators may be a sign of possession also pay attention to the frequency. It may not be possession so please be cautious, seek guidance.

The Harmful Effects of Possession

In using the term 'Possession' we include also the negative influences originating from those who are still alive in the physical plane of existence - their hateful thoughts, curses, and hexes. The worst types of possession, however, come from the invasion of 'real nasties' when protection is low from drugs or alcohol, or when the subject is unconscious - due to an accident or when under anesthetics in a hospital.

Praying on God's Armour

Prayer the chief weapon of spiritual war

BELT OF TRUTH

A Prayer for Protection

Eph 6:14

In Jesus name I claim the protection of the belt of truth; I buckle it securely around my waist. I pray the protection of the belt of truth over my personal life, my home, family and my ministry. I use the belt of truth directly against Satan and his kingdom of darkness. I aggressively embrace Christ who is the truth, as my strength and protection from all of Satan's deceptions. I desire that the truth of God's word will gain a deeper place in my life.

Forgive me for my sin of lying. Show me any way that I have been deceived by the devil. Through the Holy Spirit of truth, give me understanding of the scriptures and guide me into a practical application of its words. I ask the Holy Spirit to warn me be before I deceive anyone and to protect me from believing Satan's lies.

Thank you Lord for making me a pillar and foundation for your truth. Lord, help me to relate to and give protection and help to them through your Spirit.

Lord I see my ability to be invincible and strong despite Satan's subtle ways, because of the stabilizing power of the belt of truth. Thank you for providing this part of the armour. I accept it gratefully and desire to have an ever-deepening understanding of its protection through you power. Amen.

BREASTPLATE OF RIGHTEOUSNESS

Praying for Holy Life

Eph 6:14

Dear Jesus, I thank you for your breastplate of righteous. I denounce any dependence I may have upon my own goodness. I ask the Holy Spirit to make me righteous in action, pure in thought and have to have a holy attitude.

I hold up the righteous life of Jesus Christ to defeat Satan and his kingdom. I affirm that my victory is won and lived out by my Saviour. I eagerly ask and expect that Jesus Christ shall live his righteousness through me. Cleanse me through the precious blood of Christ and take away all my sins of omission and commission. Let me walk in a holy and clean manner that honours God and defeats the world, the flesh, and the devil through Jesus Christ, my Lord. Amen.

THE SHOES OF PEACE

A prayer for peace

Eph 6:15

Heavenly Father, by faith in the name of Jesus Christ, I put on the shoes of peace. I accept your declaration that I am justified and that I have peace with you. May my mind grasp that wondrous truth and gain ever-increasing awareness. Thank you Lord for not allowing me to have any anxiety and that I don't suffer from inner torment or turmoil.

Thank you Lord Jesus Christ for inviting me to make all of my needs known to you through prayer. Teach me to wait in your presence until the inner peace of God, which transcends human understanding, replaces my anxiety. I desire to know the strong presence of your peace. Walk with me Lord and let me hear you say, "don't be afraid; I will help you."

I want to be obedient to your will at all times. May the fullness of Christ, who is my peace, enable me to walk in him and that the fullness of his peace may glorify

God through me. I put on the shoes of peace in the name of the Lord Jesus Christ, and by faith I shall walk in them this day. Amen

The Shield of Faith

A prayer for faith

Eph 6:16

Heavenly Father I accept the protection of the shield of faith. I count upon your holy presence to surround me like a capsule, offering total protection from all of Satan's flaming arrows. Grant me the grace to accept your refining purpose in allowing some of Satan's arrows to pass through the shield, and even to praise you for it. Help me to concentrate upon your presence and not the enemy's arrows.

In Jesus name I claim the protection of the holy angels to guard and shield me from the assaults of Satan's kingdom. May these ministering angels be present to interfere with the strategy of Satan to harm my family and me? I use the victory of the blood of Jesus Christ and hold it against the advances of the evil one. With gratitude and praise, in the name of the Lord Jesus Christ, I rejoice and accept His victory. Amen.

The Helmet of Salvation

A prayer for a sound mind

Eph 6:17

Father, I accept by faith the helmet of salvation. I recognize that my salvation is in your Son, the Lord Jesus Christ. I pray that He will cover my mind with His. Let my thoughts be His thoughts. I open my mind fully and only to the control of Jesus Christ

Replace my own selfish and sinful thoughts with His. I reject every projected thought of Satan and his demons and request, instead, the mind of the Lord

Jesus Christ. Grant to me the wisdom to discern thoughts that are from the world and my old sin nature.

I praise you, Heavenly Father, for giving me the mind of Christ as I hide your word within my mind. Open my mind to love your word. Grant me with the facility and capacity to memorize large portions of it. May your word be ever my mind like a helmet of strength, which Satan cannot penetrate. Forgive me for my neglect, my failure to aggressively accept the salvation always available to me. These things I lay before you in the precious name of my saviour, Jesus Christ. Amen.

The Sword of The Spirit

A prayer for wisdom to apply Gods word

Eph 6:17

In Jesus name I take hold of the sword of the spirit, the word of God. I embrace its inerrant message of truth and power. I humbly ask the Holy Spirit to guide me into true understanding of God's word.

Grant to me the discipline and dedication to memorize the word and to saturate my mind with its truth and power.

In the name of Jesus Christ and through the Holy Ghost, grant me the wisdom so I will know how to apply the word against the enemy. Teach my spirit to use the word to defeat Satan and to advance the cause of Christ into that very realm Satan claims. Amen.

Praying In the Spirit

Praying for the out pouring of the Holy Spirit

Eph 6:18

Father, in Jesus name I ask for the spirit of God to fill me, to dwell within me and to immerse me with his power.

Lord teach me how to pray in the Spirit, tell me what words to say and how to listen to His voice. Block out any thoughts that will take my mind off you.

God make me a Prayer Warrior, equipped with all your amour and ready to intercede for others, to uplift and encourage. Give me a word for all seasons.

Lord, give me your Spirit to make me more consistent in my prayer life.

Thank you Spirit, for filling me. For the joy I experience and am yet to experience. Thanks for giving me the strength to prevail in the battle with Satan and his hosts. It's out of this victory I now live my life. It is in Jesus name we pray Amen.

References

Books
1. WOOD, S *Breaking Free: 12 Steps to Sexual Purity*
2. ANDERSON, N T The Bondage Breaker by Dr Neil T. Anderson
3. STEPHEN, A., STOEKER, F. *Every Man's Battle, Every Young Man's Battle, and Preparing your Son for Every Man's*
4. CARNES, P. *In the Shadows of the Net*
5. CARNES, P. *Out of the Shadows*
6. GROSS, G., LUFF, S. *Pure Eyes* by Craig Gross
7. WEST, C. *Theology of the Body for Beginners* by Christopher West
8. MEYER, J *Winning the Battle in your Mind*

Online Resources
1. www.fathersforgood.com: A parenting website sponsored by the Knights of Columbus
2. www.pornnomore.com: A Catholic website information, prayers and witness talks for those struggling with pornography
3. www.settingcaptivesfree.com: A Christian website addressing a number of addictions
4. www.isafe.org: A website for internet safety education
5. www.filterreview.com: A website that describes and rates different internet filters
6. www.freedomeveryday.org: A site sponsored by L.I.F.E. Ministries (Living In Freedom Everyday), a sexual addiction recovery ministry
7. www.flrl.org/truefreedom.com: A website sponsored by the Archdiocese of New York that provides resources for overcoming pornography use

RAY OF HOPE 4U CONSULTANCY

Is a Non Denominational organisation based on the belief that the needs of those requiring assistance are of utmost importance to us. Our entire team is committed to meeting needs and making people better.

Ray Patrick Is the founder, CEO of **Ray of Hope 4 U**, he has worked in schools, youth clubs, churches, prisons, cooperation's (HMS Wandsworth, NHS, Hammersmith and Fulham Council, White City Community Centre, London Borough of Brent, Seventh Day Adventist Church and London's mayoral office) and on the streets of LA (USA) and London (UK); fighting the war against drugs, Gangs and negative behaviour. Most of all Ray loves God with all his heart, soul and mind.

Our Mission: God has anointed us to bring good news to the hurt and the hurting. He has sent us to comfort the broken hearted and to let the captives know that they can be set free from their bondage mental, physical and spiritual. To bring vision to the visionless, hope to the hopeless, and help to the helpless with it, the care and love of God. Our motto is, "Not Willing That Any Should Perish"

Our Daily Purpose is to bridge the gap between faith and life so that as the individual's relationship with God grows, they begin to live a productive life. As change takes place, they experience peace and joy.

We Explore God's purpose for life. We examine our intimate relationships; we look at the emotions of anger, fear, guilt and other negative emotions within the context of the Biblical concept of love. We evaluate actions and the motives behind those actions and explore how change takes place.

OUR PROGRAMS

- Discipleship Training
- Biblical Ministries Training Program
- Biblical Counselling Certification
- Addiction Support Groups & One to One Sessions
- Biblical Life Coaching

Contact Us

Ray of Hope 4U Tel: +447429721970 **Email:**rayofhope4u@hotmail.com
website:www.rayofhope4u.co.uk & www.rayofhope4uministries.com
Facebook: Ray A Patrick   **Twitter:** rayofhope4u

Radio Broadcast: www.medianetgospel.com (worldwide)